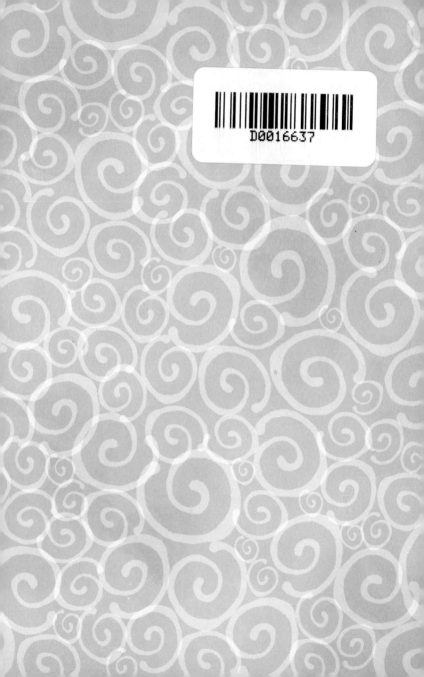

D0016637

Kindred Spirits, Forever Wacky Friends

ISBN: 978-1-59842-832-2

Wonderful Wacky Women®

Inspiring•Uplifting•Empowering

is a trademark of Suzy and Al Toronto. Used under license.

ᕼ and Blue Mountain Press are registered in U.S. Patent and Trademark Office. Certain trademarks are used under license.

Printed in China.
First Printing: 2014

❸ This book is printed on recycled paper.

This book is printed on paper that has been specially produced to be acid free (neutral pH) and contains no groundwood or unbleached pulp. It conforms with the requirements of the American National Standards Institute, Inc., so as to ensure that this book will last and be enjoyed by future generations.

Blue Mountain Arts, Inc.
P.O. Box 4549, Boulder, Colorado 80306

Kindred Spirits,
Forever Wacky Friends

Suzy Toronto

Blue Mountain Press™
Boulder, Colorado

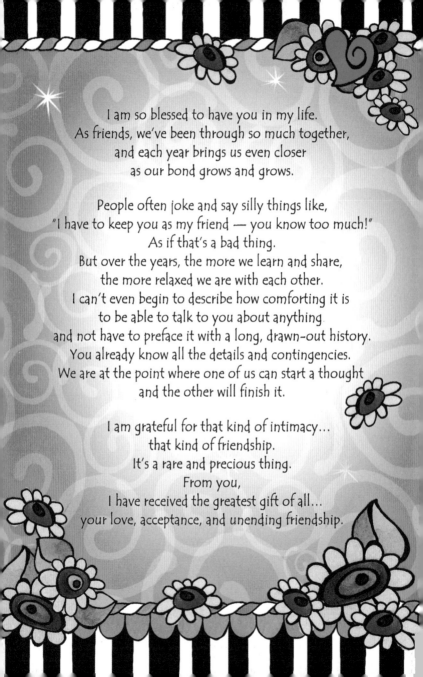

I am so blessed to have you in my life.
As friends, we've been through so much together,
and each year brings us even closer
as our bond grows and grows.

People often joke and say silly things like,
"I have to keep you as my friend — you know too much!"
As if that's a bad thing.
But over the years, the more we learn and share,
the more relaxed we are with each other.
I can't even begin to describe how comforting it is
to be able to talk to you about anything
and not have to preface it with a long, drawn-out history.
You already know all the details and contingencies.
We are at the point where one of us can start a thought
and the other will finish it.

I am grateful for that kind of intimacy…
that kind of friendship.
It's a rare and precious thing.
From you,
I have received the greatest gift of all…
your love, acceptance, and unending friendship.

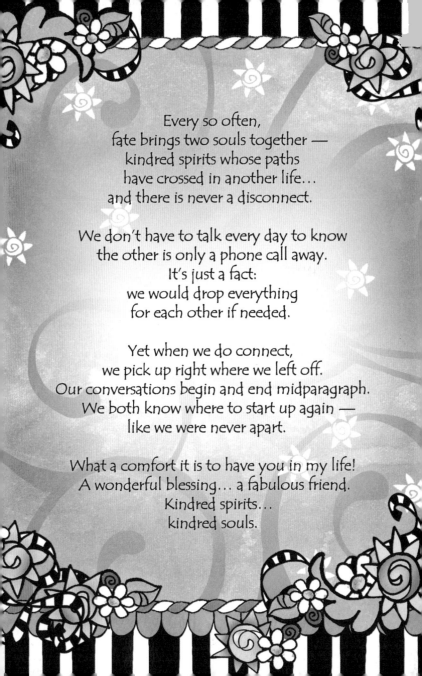

Every so often,
fate brings two souls together —
kindred spirits whose paths
have crossed in another life…
and there is never a disconnect.

We don't have to talk every day to know
the other is only a phone call away.
It's just a fact:
we would drop everything
for each other if needed.

Yet when we do connect,
we pick up right where we left off.
Our conversations begin and end midparagraph.
We both know where to start up again —
like we were never apart.

What a comfort it is to have you in my life!
A wonderful blessing… a fabulous friend.
Kindred spirits…
kindred souls.

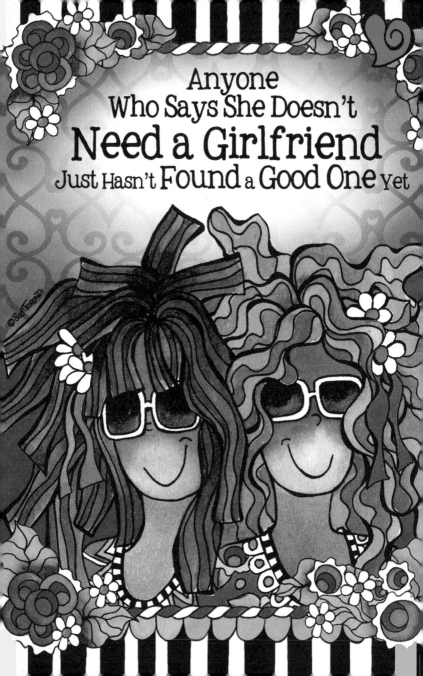

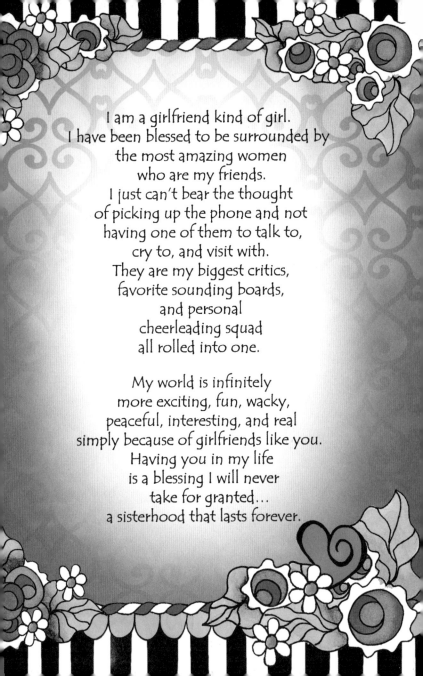

I am a girlfriend kind of girl.
I have been blessed to be surrounded by
the most amazing women
who are my friends.
I just can't bear the thought
of picking up the phone and not
having one of them to talk to,
cry to, and visit with.
They are my biggest critics,
favorite sounding boards,
and personal
cheerleading squad
all rolled into one.

My world is infinitely
more exciting, fun, wacky,
peaceful, interesting, and real
simply because of girlfriends like you.
Having you in my life
is a blessing I will never
take for granted…
a sisterhood that lasts forever.

God didn't create us with the same bloodline…
but He might as well have.
For you and I have mixed our diversity
into an eternal blend of sacred sisterhood
stronger than any natural bond.

As the finger of fate allowed our paths to cross,
we reached out and grabbed each other,
refusing to ever let go…
two wacky women clinging to each other
as if our lives depended on it.

We are sisters by choice… not by chance.

How wonderful that you get me and I get you.
We accept each other "as is"…
no apologies, no excuses, no judgments.
Whether laughing hysterically until we cry
or crying buckets of tears until we laugh,
you embrace all the goodness I have to offer,
and then, with a breath of kindness, blow the rest away.
It's the way sisterhood should be.

Maybe God did have a hand in bringing us together…
two soul mates, two friends, two eternal spirits.
Forever friends… forever sisters.

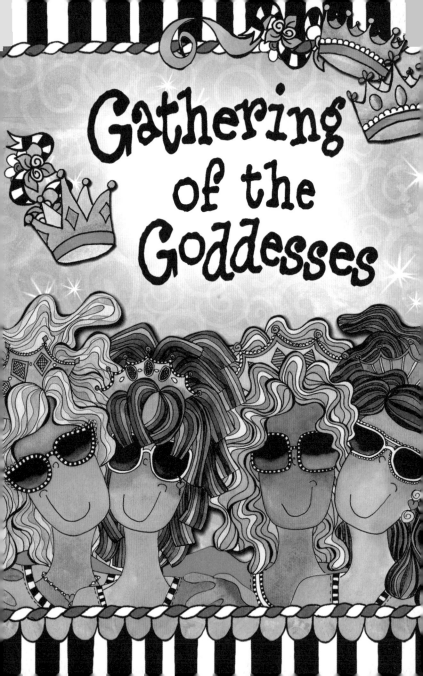

It is a known fact
that goddesses attract other goddesses.
You know, "Birds of a feather…"
But the really cool thing is that quite often
they flock together long before they reach
their true lofty status of "goddess,"
giving their friendships
the depth only time can give.
By the time they become goddesses,
they've been gathering together for so long —
giving, sharing, loving, and caring —
that they know intimate details
about one another's lives…
making their bond unbreakable.

Whether shopping, going out to lunch,
lounging over pedicures, or sitting on the beach,
a gathering of goddesses can't be missed.
Just listen for the buzz of friendship,
the tears of shared sorrows,
and the fits of irrepressible laughter.
You'll know in a minute
you're in the presence of greatness.

© Suzy Toronto

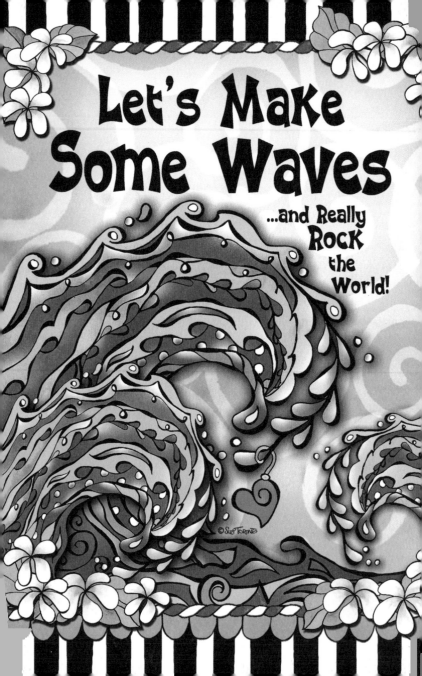

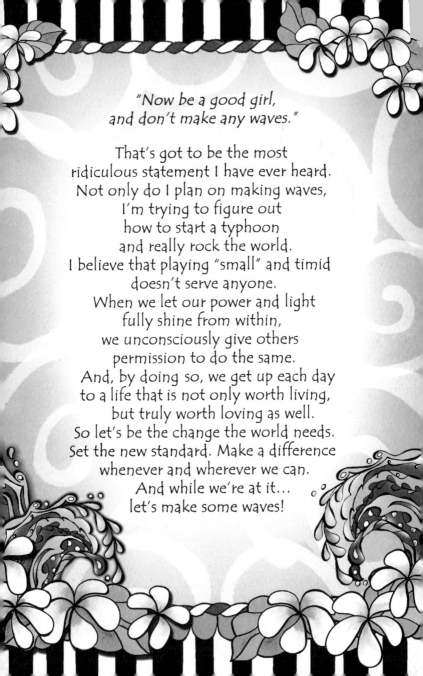

*"Now be a good girl,
and don't make any waves."*

That's got to be the most
ridiculous statement I have ever heard.
Not only do I plan on making waves,
I'm trying to figure out
how to start a typhoon
and really rock the world.
I believe that playing "small" and timid
doesn't serve anyone.
When we let our power and light
fully shine from within,
we unconsciously give others
permission to do the same.
And, by doing so, we get up each day
to a life that is not only worth living,
but truly worth loving as well.
So let's be the change the world needs.
Set the new standard. Make a difference
whenever and wherever we can.
And while we're at it...
let's make some waves!

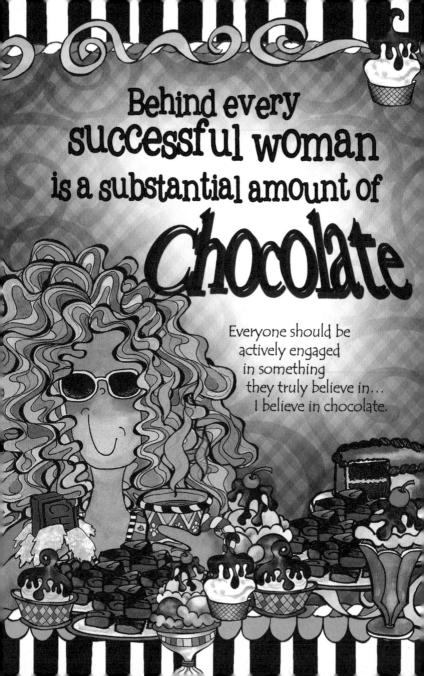

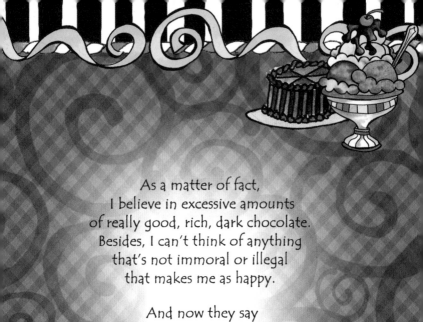

As a matter of fact,
I believe in excessive amounts
of really good, rich, dark chocolate.
Besides, I can't think of anything
that's not immoral or illegal
that makes me as happy.

And now they say
it's actually good for us!
So there you go…
it's a green light,
a legitimate excuse,
PERMISSION FROM GOD
to eat all the chocolate you want!

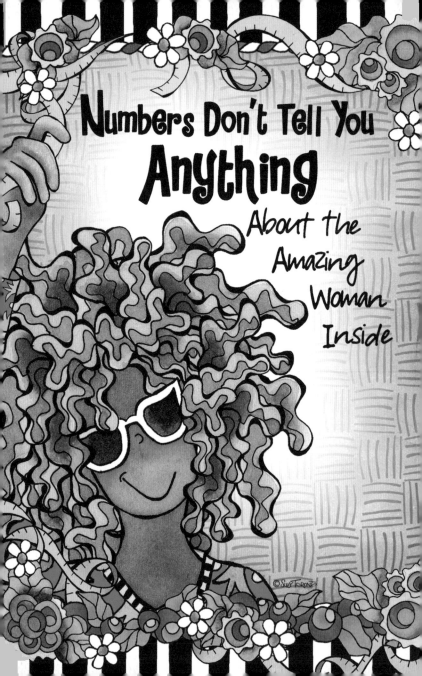

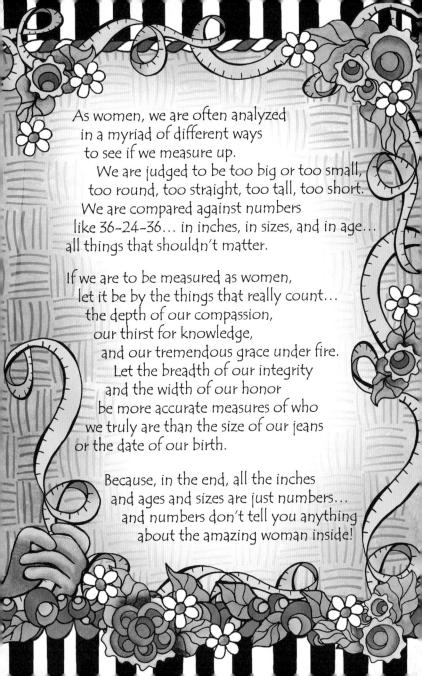

As women, we are often analyzed
in a myriad of different ways
to see if we measure up.
   We are judged to be too big or too small,
   too round, too straight, too tall, too short.
We are compared against numbers
like 36-24-36... in inches, in sizes, and in age...
all things that shouldn't matter.

If we are to be measured as women,
   let it be by the things that really count...
      the depth of our compassion,
         our thirst for knowledge,
            and our tremendous grace under fire.
            Let the breadth of our integrity
            and the width of our honor
            be more accurate measures of who
         we truly are than the size of our jeans
      or the date of our birth.

      Because, in the end, all the inches
         and ages and sizes are just numbers...
            and numbers don't tell you anything
               about the amazing woman inside!

Put On Some
Lipstick
and Go ROCK
the World

When I reflect on the women I admire who have really made a difference in this world, I like to think that before they ministered to the poor, orbited the earth, or won political office... first they put on their lipstick.

© Suzy Toronto

That small act hearkens back to a simpler time
when women showed their determination and focus
by putting on their lipstick
and then going out and doing what needed to be done.
In fact, I can remember my mother telling me to
"put on some lipstick"
before doing almost anything else —
as if this would magically give me the strength
and willpower to tackle any obstacle in my path.

And you know something? Mama was right.
Even now, when it's time to put on my big-girl panties
and dive into a new project, adventure, or challenge,
I start with a fresh face and a gorgeous shade of pink
that really makes me feel empowered.

For you, it may not be lipstick.
Maybe it's your favorite shoes or a lucky keepsake.
Maybe it's a yoga practice or a moment of meditation.
Whatever empowers you, make it part of your day.
Use what works to get your female energy moving,
and start rocking the world!

SOME OF US WERE JUST BORN WITH Glitter IN OUR VEINS

Is it genetics
or a simple fluke
of nature
that makes
some people
shine so brightly?
I think it's that
some of us
are just born
with glitter
in our veins.

© Suzy Toronto

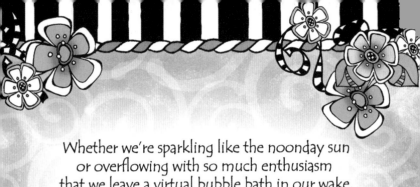

Whether we're sparkling like the noonday sun
or overflowing with so much enthusiasm
that we leave a virtual bubble bath in our wake,
the whole spectacle is out of our control.
However, it's a condition that those of us
who are affected have come to embrace.

We know that if anyone tries to dull our sparkle,
asks us to "tone it down," or suggests that we
restrain ourselves, we only have one recourse.
Grab a can of spray adhesive with one hand
and a jar of glitter with the other
and proceed to cover them with a lavish coat
of sticky, sparkly, iridescent bling.
That should do the trick!

The bottom line is that we simply
love the sparkle, glitter, and glow
that make everything around us
twinkle and shine.
Don't you?

I've pretty much decided
that when it comes to best friends,
you and I have mastered the class.
You're the kind of "bestie" that is
everything girlfriends are cracked up to be.

It's not just because we've spent so much time
laughing until we cry or just plain crying in each other's arms.
And it's not because we learned that there were no problems
or life-altering crises we couldn't face together...
with the help of a hot fudge sundae
and a box of frozen chocolate mint cookies.
It's the understanding and intuitiveness
we share all the time,
especially when life throws us
a devastating curve ball.
It's the tears of joy we share
at the most touching
and beautiful moments of our lives.
It's the look we give each other that says
"I know, and I understand,"
no matter if it's heartache or fun.

The bottom line is this:
I get you and you get me.
I know we will be forever there for each other.
For me, that really is what besties are all about.

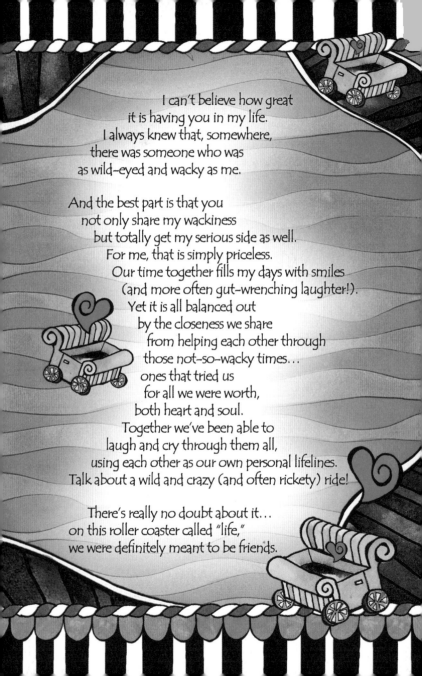

I can't believe how great
it is having you in my life.
I always knew that, somewhere,
there was someone who was
as wild-eyed and wacky as me.

And the best part is that you
not only share my wackiness
but totally get my serious side as well.
For me, that is simply priceless.
Our time together fills my days with smiles
(and more often gut-wrenching laughter!).
Yet it is all balanced out
by the closeness we share
from helping each other through
those not-so-wacky times…
ones that tried us
for all we were worth,
both heart and soul.
Together we've been able to
laugh and cry through them all,
using each other as our own personal lifelines.
Talk about a wild and crazy (and often rickety) ride!

There's really no doubt about it…
on this roller coaster called "life,"
we were definitely meant to be friends.

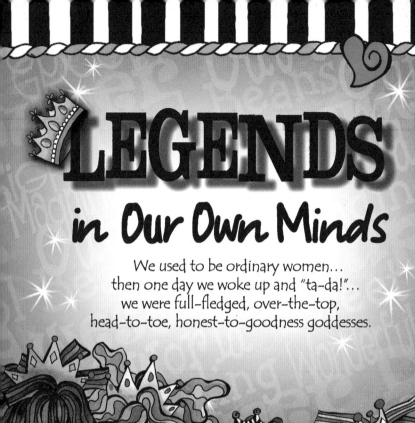

LEGENDS
in Our Own Minds

We used to be ordinary women…
then one day we woke up and "ta-da!"…
we were full-fledged, over-the-top,
head-to-toe, honest-to-goodness goddesses.

We didn't physically change on the outside,
but a magnificent transformation
took place on the inside.
Looking in the mirror,
we suddenly realized we were finally at peace
with everything about ourselves…
every curve of our bodies, every wave in our hair.
We now see ourselves as the sensuous
and radiant beings we truly are.
Oh yeah, there is no doubt about it.
We are legends in our own minds!

Top Ten Reasons Why You're Such a Great Friend

#10 You know all my history, so I don't have to explain myself when we talk.

#9 You immediately forgive my extensive and expensive shortcomings.

#8 You lift me up when I am down and knock me down when I am too full of myself.

#7 You are the president of my fan club, even though I don't have one.

#6 You tell me the truth when I ask if I look fat, and you lie when I get a bad haircut.

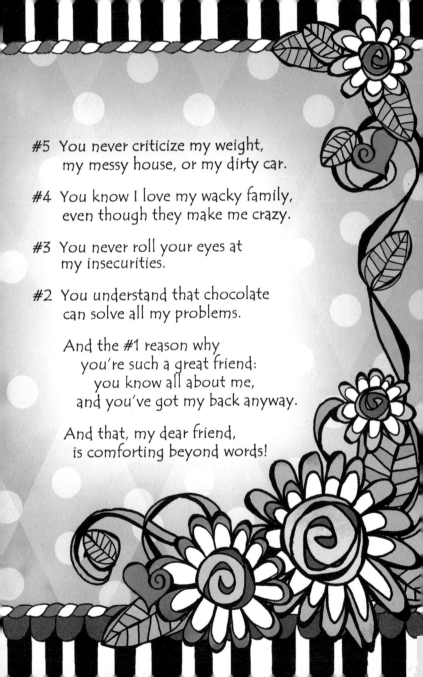

#5 You never criticize my weight,
   my messy house, or my dirty car.

#4 You know I love my wacky family,
   even though they make me crazy.

#3 You never roll your eyes at
   my insecurities.

#2 You understand that chocolate
   can solve all my problems.

And the #1 reason why
   you're such a great friend:
      you know all about me,
      and you've got my back anyway.

And that, my dear friend,
   is comforting beyond words!

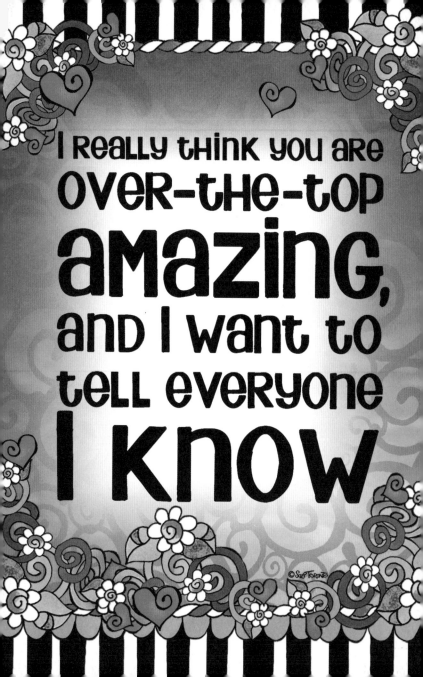

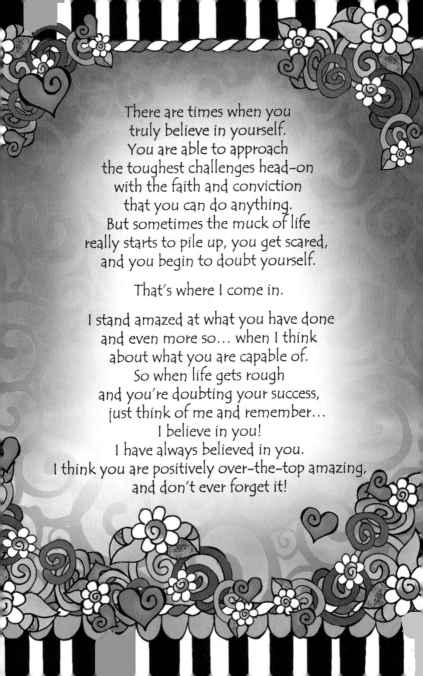

There are times when you
truly believe in yourself.
You are able to approach
the toughest challenges head-on
with the faith and conviction
that you can do anything.
But sometimes the muck of life
really starts to pile up, you get scared,
and you begin to doubt yourself.

That's where I come in.

I stand amazed at what you have done
and even more so... when I think
about what you are capable of.
So when life gets rough
and you're doubting your success,
just think of me and remember...
I believe in you!
I have always believed in you.
I think you are positively over-the-top amazing,
and don't ever forget it!

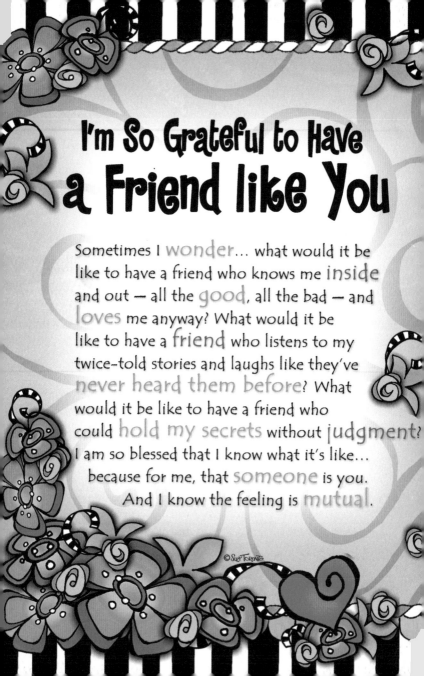

I'm So Grateful to Have a Friend like You

Sometimes I wonder... what would it be like to have a friend who knows me inside and out — all the good, all the bad — and loves me anyway? What would it be like to have a friend who listens to my twice-told stories and laughs like they've never heard them before? What would it be like to have a friend who could hold my secrets without judgment? I am so blessed that I know what it's like... because for me, that someone is you. And I know the feeling is mutual.

© Suzy Toronto

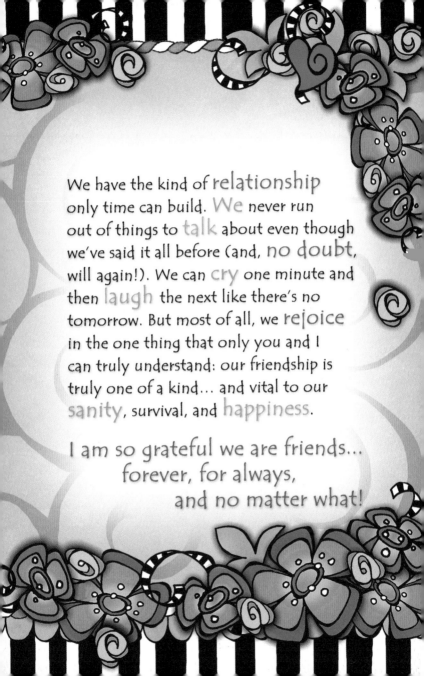

We have the kind of relationship only time can build. We never run out of things to talk about even though we've said it all before (and, no doubt, will again!). We can cry one minute and then laugh the next like there's no tomorrow. But most of all, we rejoice in the one thing that only you and I can truly understand: our friendship is truly one of a kind... and vital to our sanity, survival, and happiness.

I am so grateful we are friends... forever, for always, and no matter what!

Right from the start,
I knew our friendship was unique.
We are like yin and yang, witty and wacky,
yet we fit together so perfectly.
Over the years, our lives grew together
in some ways and apart in others,
but the bond was never broken.
The individual challenges we faced
just drew our hearts closer
as we took turns pushing each other
into the light, helping to keep
the other's priorities and perspectives.
Most important of all,
we kept our sense of humor,
always ready with a laugh or a smile
through life's greatest lessons.
What we have is unique indeed…
a friendship that has stood
the test of time.

Together… we are strong.
Together… our hearts are empowered.
Together… life is a wonderful, wacky adventure.
We are and forever will be
friends to the end!

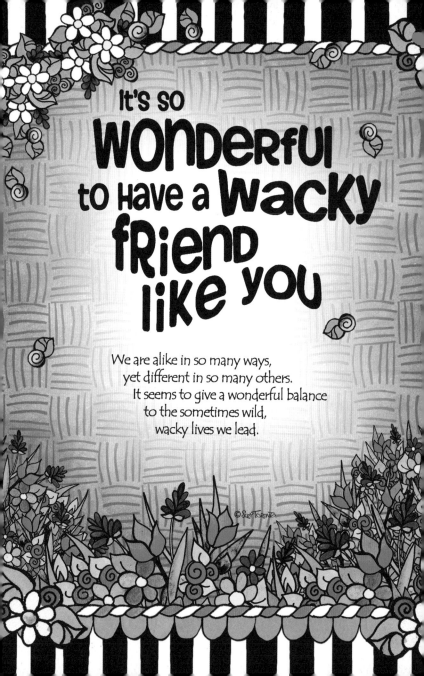

Whether we are giggling, whining, or crying,
we always seem to have a good time doing it.
We have more fun than anyone
should be allowed to,
which validates that maybe, just maybe,
our wacky lives are normal after all.

But what I really love about us are our differences.
You are strong when I am not,
you are levelheaded when I'm feeling a bit off balance,
and you lift me up when I think I can't go on.

And then, the icing on the cake...
you put up with the very worst of me
because, deep down inside, you know
the best of me is worth the hassle!

What a match we make!
Two wild, wacky, wonderful women
riding together in the front seat
of the roller coaster of life...
and having the time of our lives!

And I can't think of anyone
I'd rather do it with.

About the Author

So this is me… I'm a tad wacky and just shy of crazy. I'm fiftysomething and live in the sleepy village of Tangerine, Florida, with my husband, Al, and a big, goofy dog named Lucy. And because life wasn't crazy enough, my eightysomething-year-old parents live with us too. (In my home, the nuts don't fall far from the tree!) I eat far too much chocolate, and I drink sparkling water by the gallon. I practice yoga, ride a little red scooter, and go to the beach every chance I get. I have five grown children and over a dozen grandkids who love me as much as I adore them. I teach them to dip their French fries in their chocolate shakes and to make up any old words to the tunes they like. But most of all, I teach them to never, ever color inside the lines. This is the Wild Wacky Wonderful life I lead, and I wouldn't have it any other way. Welcome to my world!

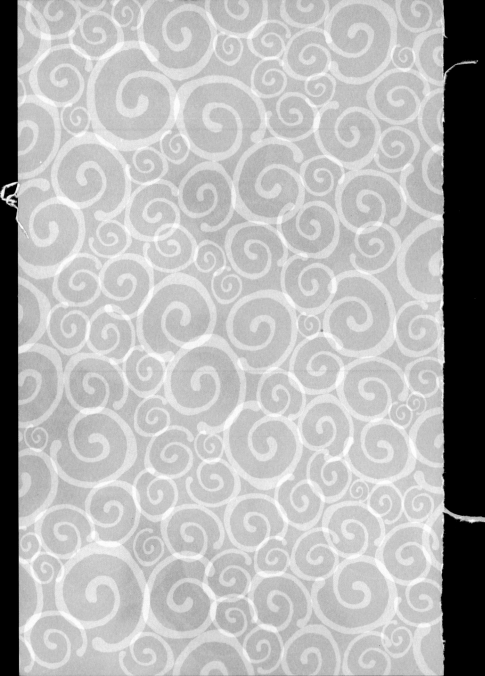